Design: Judith Chant and Alison Lee
Recipe Photography: Peter Barry
Jacket and Illustration Artwork: Jane Winton, courtesy of
Bernard Thornton Artists, London
Editors: Jillian Stewart and Kate Cranshaw

CLB 4260
Published by Grange Books, an imprint of Grange Books PLC,
The Grange, Grange Yard, London, SE1 3AG
© 1995 CLB Publishing, Godalming, Surrey, England.
All rights reserved
Printed and bound in Singapore
Published 1995
ISBN 1-85627-568-X

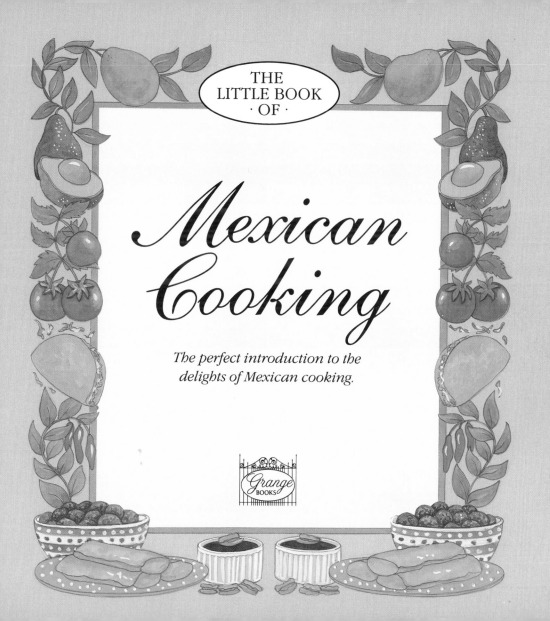

THE LITTLE BOOK · OF ·

Mexican Cooking

The perfect introduction to the delights of Mexican cooking.

Grange
BOOKS

Introduction

Mexican food awakens the taste buds and is a particularly enjoyable and exciting way of entertaining. If you are unfamiliar with Mexican cooking, then embrace it as an uncomplicated and stimulating new addition to your culinary repertoire. The flavours are flamboyant and distinctive, and the shapes are interesting, too, with many varying little parcels, rolls and envelopes filled with piquant surprises, which are handed round with fiery dips and crisp salad.

In Mexico the tortilla is generally the base to all savoury foods, and is the wrapping that encloses the meat, vegetables, beans and cheese, or whatever is locally available. Tortillas are unleavened rounds of bread, made of maize in the south of Mexico and wheat in the north. They are rolled into flat pancakes and baked on a hot griddle. Tortillas are mentioned frequently in these recipes and appear in many different guises: for Enchiladas tortillas are filled, rolled, covered with a sauce and then baked; for Chimichangas tortillas are filled and then fried; and for Tacos the tortillas are first fried and then filled. They are delicious, too, when served warmed to accompany a meat or vegetable main dish. Mexican food is increasing in popularity and wheat tortillas can now be purchased in supermarkets, along with some of the other staples such as tacos, tortilla chips and tostadas.

These plain unleavened-bread bases are used as a foil for the sharp and fiery all Mexican tastes of chillies, green peppers, spring onions, lime juice and garlic. These are the key ingredients without which the end effect is not authentic. Of course, all these can be adjusted to suit individual tastes. In Mexico, as in most countries of the world that enjoy a warm climate, the food is spicy. The addition of spices to food cooked in these climates has a two-fold purpose: they act as a preservative while also stimulating appetites flagging in the heat. Spicy food need not necessarily be hot, though. Cumin, coriander and cinnamon are favourite choices in Mexico and lend their flavour without bringing tears to the eyes. For those who like things hot, fresh or dried chilli peppers or cayenne pepper will add fire to any dish. Chillies in particular do vary in strength and should be used with some caution. Cocoa is another important Mexican ingredient which appears, surprisingly, in both savoury and sweet dishes and gives a depth of colour and flavour to meat dishes without making them taste of chocolate!

This book contains an exciting mixture of some of Mexico's most famous dishes and is the perfect introduction to this tasty cuisine, as well as a springboard from which the competent cook can go on to create his or her own Mexican-style recipes.

Guacamole

SERVES 8

This is one of Mexico's most famous dishes. It is delicious as a first course on its own or as an ingredient in other recipes.

PREPARATION: 25 mins

1 medium onion, finely chopped
1 clove garlic, crushed
Grated zest and juice of ½ lime
½ quantity Taco Sauce (see recipe)
3 large ripe avocados
Salt and black pepper
1 tbsp chopped fresh coriander
Coriander leaves, to garnish
Tortilla chips, to serve

1. Mix the onion, garlic, zest and juice of the lime and the taco sauce together in a large bowl.

2. Cut the avocados in half lengthways. Twist the halves gently in opposite directions to separate.

Step 2 Cut the avocados in half lengthways and twist the halves in opposite directions to separate.

Step 3 Hit the stone with a large knife and twist to remove.

3. Hit the stone with the blade of a large, sharp knife and twist the knife to remove the stone.

4. Place the avocado halves cut side down on a chopping board. Lightly score the skin lengthwise and gently pull back to peel. Alternatively, scoop out avocado flesh with a spoon, scraping the skin well.

5. Chop the avocado roughly and immediately place in the bowl with the onion and lime.

6. Use a potato masher to break up the avocado until almost smooth. Do not over-mash. Season, and stir in the chopped coriander. Spoon into a serving bowl and garnish with coriander leaves.

7. Surround the bowl with tortilla chips for dipping.

Burritos

SERVES 6

In Mexico this dish is very popular, beans are the traditional filling, but meat may be used as well.

PREPARATION: 25 mins
COOKING: 20 mins

6 Flour Tortillas (see recipe)
1 onion, chopped
1 tbsp oil
460g/1lb canned refried beans
6 lettuce leaves, shredded
120g/4oz Cheddar cheese, grated
2 tomatoes, sliced
2 tbsps snipped chives
Full quantity Taco Sauce recipe
140ml/¼ pint soured cream
Chopped coriander leaves

1. Wrap the tortillas in foil and heat in a warm oven to soften them.

2. Cook the onion in the oil until soft but not coloured. Add the beans and heat through.

3. Spoon the mixture down the centre of each

Step 3 Fold in the ends and sides of each tortilla over the filling to make rectangular parcels.

warm tortilla. Top with the lettuce, cheese, tomatoes and chives. Fold over the sides to form long rectangular parcels. Make sure the filling is completely enclosed.

4. Place the burritos in an ovenproof dish, cover and cook in an oven preheated to 180°C/350°F/Gas Mark 4, for about 20 minutes.

5. Spoon over the hot taco sauce. Top with the soured cream and sprinkle with chopped coriander to serve.

Moyettes

SERVES 4

While these sandwiches make excellent lunch fare, they are very popular for breakfast in Mexico.

PREPARATION: 15 mins
COOKING: 20 mins

---

4 crusty rolls
30g/1oz butter or margarine
225g/8oz canned refried beans
2 spring onions, chopped
30g/4 tbsps grated Tilsit cheese

---

1. Cut the rolls in half and remove some of the insides.

Step 1 Remove some of the insides of each roll using a teaspoon or small knife.

Step 3 Fill the bottom halves of the rolls with the refried beans.

2. Soften the butter and spread on the insides of the rolls.

3. Fill the bottom halves of the rolls with the refried beans.

4. Sprinkle with the spring onion and top with the grated cheese then the bread 'lids'.

5. Place the rolls on a baking sheet and cook in an oven preheated to 160°C/325°F/Gas Mark 3, for 15-20 minutes, or until the cheese has melted and the beans are hot. Serve immediately.

Chimichangas

SERVES 6

A strange sounding name for a delicious snack which is something like a deep-fried taco.

PREPARATION: 30 mins
COOKING: 18 mins

6 Flour Tortillas (see recipe)
Half quantity Chilli Con Carne recipe
6 lettuce leaves, shredded
6 spring onions, chopped
90g/3oz Cheddar cheese, grated
Oil, for frying
Half quantity Guacamole recipe
140ml/¼ pint soured cream
1 tomato, seeded and chopped

1. Wrap the tortillas in foil and place in a warm oven for 5 minutes to make them pliable.

2. Heat the chilli briefly and spoon about 2

Step 3 Fold the tortillas over the filling to enclose completely and form parcels.

Step 4 Lower the parcels into the hot oil folded side first.

tbsps onto the centre of each tortilla. Top with the lettuce, spring onions and cheese.

3. Fold in the sides to make parcels making sure all the filling is enclosed.

4. Heat about 2.5cm/1-inch of oil in a large frying pan and when hot, lower in the chimichangas folded side down first. Cook 2-4 at a time depending on the size of the pan.

5. Cook for 3 minutes and carefully turn over. Cook a further 3 minutes, remove to kitchen paper and drain. Repeat with the remaining chimichangas.

6. Spoon the guacamole over the top of each and drizzle over the soured cream. Sprinkle over the chopped tomato and serve immediately.

Nachos

SERVES 8-10

These make excellent cocktail savouries and the variety of toppings and flavour combinations is almost endless.

PREPARATION: 20 mins
COOKING: 25 mins

Beef filling
2 tsps oil
225g/8oz minced beef
½ onion, chopped
1-2 tsps chilli powder
Pinch of ground coriander
Pinch of cayenne pepper
Salt and pepper

1 pack round tortilla chips
1 can refried beans
Full quantity Taco Sauce recipe
1 can Jalapeño bean dip
8-10 cherry tomatoes, sliced
120ml/4 fl oz soured cream or natural yogurt
Black and stuffed green olives, sliced
Cheddar cheese, grated

1. Heat the oil for the beef filling in a frying pan and brown the mince and onion, breaking the meat up as it cooks. Add the spices and seasoning and cook for about 20 minutes.

2. Top half of the tortilla chips with the refried beans and half with the beef filling.

3. Place a spoonful of taco sauce on the bean-topped chips and Jalapeño bean dip in the beef-topped chips.

4. Top the nachos with tomatoes, soured cream or yogurt, olives or cheese in any combination, and serve.

Step 4 Top the nachos with tomatoes, soured cream, olives or cheese, as preferred and serve.

Taco Sauce

MAKES 280ml/½ pint

This basic recipe has many uses in Mexican cooking – sauce, topping, dip or as an ingredient to give a dish extra flavour.

PREPARATION: 20 mins
COOKING: 10 mins

1 tbsp oil
1 onion, diced
1 green pepper, diced
½-1 red or green chilli
½ tsp ground cumin
½ tsp ground coriander
1 clove garlic, crushed
Pinch of salt, pepper and sugar
400g/14oz can tomatoes
Tomato purée (optional)

1. Heat the oil in a heavy-based saucepan and when hot, add the onion and pepper. Cook slowly to soften slightly.

2. Chop the chilli and add with the cumin, coriander and garlic and cook a further 2-3 minutes.

3. Add sugar, seasonings and the tomatoes with their juice.

4. Cook for a further 5-6 minutes over a

Step 2 Cut the chilli in half, removing the seeds if wished, and chop the flesh finely.

Step 3 Add the sugar, seasonings and the tomatoes to the pan and use a fork or wooden spoon to break up the tomatoes.

moderate heat to reduce and thicken slightly. Add the tomato purée for colour, if necessary. Adjust the seasoning and use hot or cold according to your recipe.

Flour Tortillas

MAKES 12

Tortillas made with wheat instead of corn are traditional in northern Mexico. Flour tortillas are easier to make and use than the corn variety.

PREPARATION: 60 mins
COOKING: 5 mins

460g/1lb plain flour
1 tbsp salt
90g/3oz lard or white vegetable fat
About 280ml/½ pint hot water

---

1. Sift the flour and salt into a mixing bowl and rub in the lard until the mixture resembles fine breadcrumbs. Gradually mix in enough of the water to form a soft, pliable dough.

2. Knead on a well-floured surface until smooth and no longer sticky. Cover with a damp tea-towel.

Step 2 Knead the dough on a floured surface until smooth and pliable.

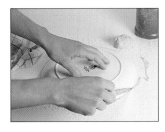

Step 4 Roll each ball of dough out very thinly and cut out a 25cm/10-inch circle.

3. Cut off about 3 tbsps of dough at a time, keeping the rest covered. Knead into a ball.

4. Roll the ball of dough out into a very thin circle with a floured rolling pin. Cut into a neat round using a 25 cm/10-inch plate as a guide. Continue until all the dough is used.

5. Stack the tortillas as you make them, flouring each well to prevent sticking. Cover with a clean tea-towel.

6. Heat a large heavy-based frying pan and carefully place in a tortilla. Cook for about 10 seconds per side. Stack and keep covered until all are cooked. Use according to chosen recipe.

Tacos

MAKES 12
Ready-made taco shells make this famous Mexican snack easy to prepare.

PREPARATION: 40 mins
COOKING: 20 mins

12 taco shells

Beef filling
Double quantity beef filling recipe for Nachos

Chicken filling
45g/1½oz butter or margarine
1 onion, chopped
1 small red pepper, chopped
340g/12oz chicken finely chopped
1 piece fresh root ginger, chopped
90ml/6 tbsps milk mixed with 2 tsps cornflour
120ml/4 fl oz soured cream
2 tbsps flaked almonds, toasted

Toppings
Shredded lettuce, grated cheese and Taco
   Sauce (see recipe)

1. Prepare the beef filling as for the Nachos recipe.

2. For the chicken filling, melt 30g/1oz of the butter in a pan and add the onion and pepper. Cook until softened.

3. Add the remaining butter to the pan and cook the chicken for 5 minutes, turning often. Season and return the onion mixture to the pan along with the chopped ginger.

4. Stir in the milk mixture. Bring to the boil and stir until very thick. Mix in the soured cream and almonds and cook gently to heat through. Do not boil.

5. Heat the taco shells on a baking sheet, open ends down, in an oven preheated to 180°C/350°F/Gas Mark 4, for 2-3 minutes.

6. To fill, spoon in about 1 tbsp of beef or chicken filling. Add some shredded lettuce, and some grated cheese then top with taco sauce.

Prawns Veracruz

SERVES 4-6

Veracruz is a port on the Gulf of Mexico which lends its name to a variety of colourful seafood dishes.

PREPARATION: 25 mins
COOKING: 15 mins

1 tbsp oil
1 onion, chopped
1 large green pepper, cut into 4cm/1½-inch strips
2-3 green chillies, seeded and chopped
Double quantity Taco Sauce recipe
2 tomatoes, skinned and roughly chopped
12 pimento-stuffed olives, halved
2 tsps capers
¼ tsp ground cumin
Salt
460g/1lb raw, peeled prawns
Juice of 1 lime
Boiled rice, to serve

1. Heat the oil in a large frying pan and add the onion and green pepper. Cook until soft but not coloured.

Step 2 Add the chillies, taco sauce, tomatoes, olives, capers, cumin and salt to the pan. Bring to the boil.

2. Add the chillies, taco sauce, tomatoes, olives, capers, cumin and salt. Bring to the boil and then lower the heat to simmer for 5 minutes.

3. Remove the black veins, if present, from the rounded side of the prawns with a cocktail stick.

4. Add the prawns to the sauce and cook until they curl up and turn pink and opaque. Add the lime juice to taste and serve with boiled rice.

Enchiladas

SERVES 6

Although fillings and sauces vary, enchiladas (stuffed rolled tortillas) are one of the tastiest Mexican dishes. Serve with guacamole or refried beans.

PREPARATION: 30 mins
COOKING: 20 mins

10 ripe tomatoes, skinned, seeded and chopped
1 small onion, chopped
1-2 chillies, seeded and chopped
1 clove garlic, crushed
1-2 tbsps tomato purée
30g/1oz butter or margarine
2 eggs
225ml/8 fl oz double cream
340g/12oz minced pork
1 small red pepper, chopped
30g/4 tbsps each raisins and pine nuts
12 Flour Tortillas (see recipe)
30g/4 tbsps grated cheese
Sliced spring onions, to garnish

1. Place first five ingredients into a blender or food processor and purée until smooth. Melt the butter in a large pan. Add the purée mixture and simmer for 5 minutes.

2. Beat together the eggs and cream, mixing well. Add some of the hot purée and mix quickly. Return the mixture to the pan. Heat slowly, stirring constantly, until the mixture thickens. Do not boil.

3. Cook the pork and pepper slowly in a large frying pan. Turn up the heat when the pork is nearly cooked and fry briskly for a few minutes. Add the raisins, nuts and seasoning.

4. Combine about ¼ of the sauce with the meat and spoon onto one side of the centre of each tortilla. Roll up the tortillas around it, leaving the ends open and some of the filling showing.

5. Place the enchiladas seam side down in a baking dish and pour over the remaining sauce, leaving the ends uncovered. Sprinkle over the cheese and bake in an oven preheated to 180°C/350°F/Gas Mark 4, for 15-20 minutes, or until bubbling. Sprinkle with spring onions and serve immediately.

Chilli con Carne

SERVES 4

Although this dish is Mexican in origin, the version everyone knows best is really more American.

PREPARATION: 15 mins
COOKING: 40 mins

1 tbsp oil
460g/1lb minced beef
2 tsps ground cumin
2 tsps mild or hot chilli powder
Pinch oregano
Salt, pepper and pinch sugar
¼ tsp garlic powder
2 tbsps flour
460g/1lb canned tomatoes
460g/1lb canned red kidney beans
Boiled rice, to serve

1. Heat the oil in a large saucepan and brown the meat, breaking it up with a fork as it cooks.

2. Sprinkle on the cumin, chilli powder, oregano, salt, pepper and sugar, garlic and flour. Cook, stirring frequently, over a medium heat for about 3 minutes.

3. Add the tomatoes and their liquid and

Step 2 Sprinkle the spice mixture over the browned meat.

Step 3 Add the tomatoes and their liquid to the pan. Use a large spoon or potato masher to break them up.

simmer for 25-30 minutes.

4. Drain the kidney beans and add just before serving, heating through for about 5 minutes. Serve with hot boiled rice.

Flautas

SERVES 6

Traditionally, these are long, thin rolls of tortillas with savoury fillings, topped with soured cream.

PREPARATION: 60 mins
COOKING: 30 mins

---

12 Flour Tortillas (see recipe)
225g/8oz chicken, skinned, boned and minced
   or finely chopped
1 tbsp oil
1 small onion, finely chopped
½ green pepper, finely chopped
½-1 chilli, seeded and finely chopped
90g/3oz frozen sweetcorn, defrosted
6 black olives, pitted and chopped
120ml/4 fl oz double cream
Salt
Taco Sauce, Guacamole (see recipes) and
   soured cream, for toppings

---

1. Wrap the tortillas in foil and place in a warm oven for 5 minutes to make them pliable.

2. Heat the oil in a medium frying pan and add the chicken, onion and green pepper. Cook over a moderate heat, stirring frequently to break up the pieces of chicken.

3. When the chicken is cooked and the

Step 4 Roll up the tortillas and secure with cocktail sticks.

vegetables are softened, add the chilli, sweetcorn, olives, cream and salt. Bring to the boil over a high heat and boil rapidly, stirring continuously to reduce and thicken the cream.

4. Place 2 tortillas on a clean work surface, overlapping them by about 5cm/2 inches. Spoon some of the chicken mixture onto the tortillas, roll up and secure with wooden cocktail sticks. Repeat process.

5. Fry the flautas in about 1.25cm/½ inch oil in a large frying pan. Do not allow the tortillas to get very brown. Drain on kitchen paper.

6. Arrange the flautas on plates and top with soured cream, guacamole and taco sauce.

Leg of Lamb with Chilli Sauce

SERVES 4
Give Sunday roast lamb a Mexican taste with a spicy orange sauce.

PREPARATION: 15 mins, plus 12-24 hours for the lamb to marinate
COOKING: 2 hours 20 mins

1kg/2¼lb leg of lamb
1 tbsp cornflour mixed with 2 tbsps water
Orange slices and coriander to garnish

Marinade
1 tsp cocoa powder
½ tsp cayenne pepper
½ tsp ground cumin
½ tsp paprika
½ tsp ground oregano
140ml/¼ pint water
140ml/¼ pint orange juice
140ml/¼ pint red wine
1 clove of garlic, crushed
2 tbsps brown sugar

1. Mix together the marinade ingredients, and pour over the lamb, turning it to coat. Cover and refrigerate for 12-24 hours, turning occasionally.

2. Drain the lamb, reserving the marinade, and place in a roasting tin. Cook, basting occasionally with the marinade, in an oven preheated to 180°C/350°F/Gas Mark 4, for about 2 hours or until cooked to taste.

3. Remove the lamb to a serving dish and keep warm. Skim off the fat from the roasting tin. Pour remaining marinade into the tin and bring to the boil, stirring.

4. Add some of the hot liquid to the cornflour mixture then gradually stir into the pan and bring back to the boil. Cook, stirring constantly, until thickened and clear. Add some water if necessary.

5. Garnish the lamb with orange slices and sprigs of coriander. Pour over some of the sauce and serve the rest separately.

Tostadas

MAKES 12
These are popular all over Mexico and the toppings reflect the food available in each area.
They are delicious, but difficult to eat!

PREPARATION: 40 mins
COOKING: 15 mins

2 tsps oil
460g/1lb minced beef or pork
2 tsps chilli powder
1 tsp ground cumin
1 tsp ground coriander
1 can refried beans
1 pack tostada shells

Toppings
Shredded lettuce
Grated Cheddar cheese
Tomatoes, seeded and chopped
Soured cream
Olives
Cooked, peeled prawns
Spring onions, chopped
Taco Sauce (see recipe)

1. Heat the oil in a medium frying pan. Add the mince and fry quickly to brown, then cook over a moderate heat for 8-10 minutes. Sprinkle on the spices and cook for 1-2 minutes.

2. Reheat the beans and place the tostada shells on a baking sheet. Heat for 2-3 minutes in a moderate oven.

3. Spread 1-2 tbsps of the beans on each tostada shell.

4. Top each shell with some of the beef mixture.

5. Add the topping ingredients in different combinations and serve immediately.

Step 4 Spoon some beef mixture over the beans, pushing it down gently.

Minute Steaks with Taco Sauce

SERVES 6

Prepare the sauce in advance and keep it on hand to add last-minute spice to a meal.

PREPARATION: 15 mins
COOKING: 30 mins

Full quantity Taco Sauce recipe
30g/1oz butter or margarine
2 tbsps oil
6 minute steaks
Salt and pepper
120g/4oz button mushrooms, left whole
Chopped parsley or coriander leaves

1. Prepare the taco sauce according to the recipe. Heat the butter and oil together in a large frying pan.

Step 2 Sauté the steaks for 2-3 minutes on each side or until cooked to taste.

Step 3 Add the whole mushrooms to the pan and sautée until lightly browned.

2. Season the steaks with salt and pepper and fry two or three at a time for 2-3 minutes on each side, or to taste.

3. Remove the steaks to a warm serving dish and add the mushrooms to the pan. Sauté over a high heat to brown lightly, remove and keep warm.

4. Drain most of the fat from the pan and pour in the taco sauce. Place over a low heat until just bubbling. Spoon over the steaks.

5. Top the steaks with the sautéed mushrooms and sprinkle over some parsley or coriander before serving.

Mexican Chocolate Flan

SERVES 4

Flan in Mexico is a moulded custard with a caramel sauce. Chocolate and cinnamon is a favourite flavour combination.

PREPARATION: 30 mins
COOKING: 40 mins, plus overnight chilling

120g/4oz caster sugar
2 tbsps water
Juice of ½ lime
60g/2oz plain chocolate
280ml/½ pint milk
1 cinnmamon stick
2 whole eggs
2 egg yolks
60g/4 tbsps sugar

1. Combine the first amount of sugar with the water and lime juice in a small, heavy-based saucepan.

2. Cook over a gentle heat, stirring until the sugar dissolves, then without stirring, bring the syrup to the boil and cook until golden brown and caramelised.

3. While preparing the syrup, heat 4 ramekins in an oven preheated to 180°C/350°F/Gas Mark 4. When the syrup is ready, pour into the hot ramekins and swirl to coat the sides and base evenly. Leave to cool at room temperature.

4. Chop the chocolate into small pieces and heat with the milk and cinnamon, stirring occasionally to help the chocolate dissolve.

5. Whisk the whole eggs and the yolks together with the remaining sugar until slightly frothy. Gradually whisk in the hot chocolate milk. Remove the cinnamon stick.

6. Strain the chocolate custard carefully into the ramekins and stand them in a roasting tin filled with enough hand-hot water to come half way up the sides of the dishes.

7. Carefully place the roasting tin in the oven, and bake the custards for 20-25 minutes, or until they have just set, and a knife inserted in the centre of the custard comes out clean.

8. Cool at room temperature and refrigerate for several hours or overnight before serving. Loosen the custards by running a knife around the edges and invert onto individual serving plates. If necessary shake the custard to allow it to drop out.

Tropical Fruit Salad

SERVES 6

A refreshing mixture of exotic fruits is the most popular sweet in Mexico. Add tequila or triple sec to the syrup for a special occasion.

PREPARATION: 45 mins

½ cantaloupe or honeydew melon, cubed or made into balls
½ small fresh pineapple, peeled, cored and cubed or sliced
120g/4oz fresh strawberries, hulled and halved (leave whole, if small)
1 mango, peeled and sliced or cubed
225g/8oz watermelon, seeded and cubed
120g/4oz guava or papaya, peeled and cubed
2 oranges, peeled and segmented
1 prickly pear, peeled and sliced (optional)
120g/4oz caster sugar
120ml/4 fl oz water
Grated zest and juice of 1 lime
2 tbsps chopped pecans, to decorate

1. To make melon balls, cut the melon in half and scoop out seeds and discard them. To use a melon baller, press the cutting edge firmly into the melon flesh and twist around to scoop out round pieces.

2. It is easier to core the pineapple if it is first

Step 2 Cut the pineapple into quarters and remove the core with a serrated knife.

cut into quarters. Use a serrated fruit knife to cut the point off the quarter, removing the core. Slice off the peel and remove any brown 'eyes' with the end of a peeler. Cut into slices or cubes and mix with the other fruit.

3. Dissolve the sugar in the water over a gentle heat and when the mixture is no longer grainy, bring to the boil and cook for 1 minute, then leave it to cool completely.

4. Add the lime zest and juice to the sugar syrup and pour over the prepared fruit. Refrigerate well before serving, then sprinkle with the chopped nuts.

Mango Fool

SERVES 6
To cool the palate after a spicy Mexican meal, the taste of mango, lime, ginger and cream is perfect.

PREPARATION: 20 mins, plus chilling

2 ripe mangoes
1 small piece fresh root ginger, peeled and shredded
120g/4oz icing sugar, sifted
Juice of ½ lime
140ml/¼ pint double cream

1. Cut the mangoes in half, cutting either side of the large central stone. Reserve two slices,

Step 1 Cut the mangoes in half slicing around the large central stone and scoop out the flesh.

Step 3 Whip the cream until soft peaks form.

then scoop out the flesh into a bowl, blender or food processor.

2. Add the ginger, icing sugar and lime juice and purée in the blender or food processor until smooth.

3. Whip the cream until soft peaks form and then fold into the mango purée.

4. Divide the mixture between 6 glass serving dishes and leave in the refrigerator for 1 hour before serving.

5. Cut the reserved mango slices into 6 smaller slices or pieces and use to decorate the fool.

Index